And if You Can't

Written by: Sydney Hatcher
Illustrations by: Bella Bartlett
& Sydney Hatcher

Written two years too late
for my daughter in heaven.

The last story I wish I could have read to you.

Love,
Mommy

Run, darling!
Run as fast as the stream flows.

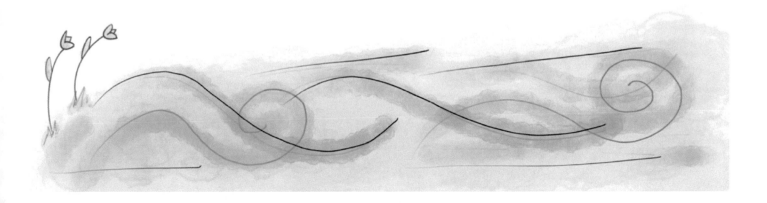

And if you can't...

I'll run for you.

Leap, my love!

Leap over the water that pools
into puddles along the path.

And if you can't,
I'll leap for you.

Skip, sweetie!

Skip joyfully to the song of the
rustling leaves in the trees
that house the birds
all bursting with tunes
composed just for you!

And if you can't,
I'll skip for you.

Reach, my child!

Reach up through the branches
that form a sturdy ladder
for you to climb about.

And if you can't,
I'll reach for you.

Look, little one!

Look at the view of the streams
and the puddles
and the leaves
and the birds
all knit together like art.

And if you can't,
I'll look for you.

Breathe, my dear!

Breathe in the blooms-bursting
with berries,
sweeter than honey in tea!

And if you can't,
I'll breathe for you.

Be.
Sweet one, just be.
As you are, still and beautiful.

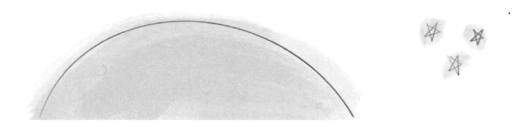

And if you can't,
I'll be for you.

Stay, my baby.

Stay as long as you can.
And I'll sing to you of the streams,
and the puddles,
and the leaves, birds, and blooms...

And if you can't,
don't wait for me.

Where you are going is more beautiful
than all I can show you.

You'll run faster, leap longer,
skip stronger, reach higher,
look further, breathe easier,
be perfect.

When you get to where you're going,
run to the most beautiful tree
with the most beautiful view!

You'll be able to see far
my little one...

maybe you'll be able

to see me.

And if you can't,
please know...

I'll be running baby, running fast for you.

I'll be leaping over tears.
I'll skip strong in your spirit.

I'll be reaching up to the heavens,
day and night until I hold you again.

I'll look for you in each bloom,
wondering how you've grown.

I'll be breathing,
one short breath at a time...

I'll be here...

Wishing you could stay...

And if you can't,

it's okay...

my love will
reach you
anyway.

Made in the USA
Middletown, DE
10 September 2020